Twenty to M...

Mini
Sugar Shoes

Frances McNaughton

Search Press

First published in Great Britain 2012

Search Press Limited
Wellwood, North Farm Road,
Tunbridge Wells, Kent TN2 3DR

Reprinted 2013

Text copyright © Frances McNaughton 2012

Photographs by Debbie Patterson at
Search Press Studios

Photographs and design copyright
© Search Press Ltd 2012

Print ISBN: 978-1-84448-844-5
Epub ISBN: 978-1-78126-050-0
Mobi ISBN: 978-1-78126-104-0
PDF ISBN: 978-1-78126-158-3

Suppliers

If you have difficulty in obtaining any of the
materials and equipment mentioned in this book,
then please visit the Search Press website for
details of suppliers: www.searchpress.com

Printed in Malaysia

Dedication

*To Mike, Annie and Anne for their
constant support.*

Contents

Introduction

Shoes have been a fashionable decoration on cakes for quite a long time but, with the increase in embellishments for cupcakes, these tiny shoes have become very popular.

The shoes shown here have taken on a life of their own since I developed the method of using squares and circles to cut the various pieces for the shoes several years ago. Using cutters when making such tiny models helps with the shaping, as it minimises the amount of handling needed. Templates for the soles are included below for those who prefer to work from scratch.

The methods shown here can all be expanded to add tiny adjustments of your own using different embossers, cutters and colours to design your own shoes. As they are so small, they are relatively quick to make, and do not need to be made with very much detail. Why not personalise each shoe with your own initial? I painted the 'F' on some of the shoes using pearl or metallic powder food colours mixed with alcohol, using a very fine brush.

Although I made the shoes in sugar for this book, the methods could easily be adapted for use with other, non-edible, modelling media; for example polymer clay and air-drying clay. Fans of dolls' houses could also make use of them.

I hope you have fun.

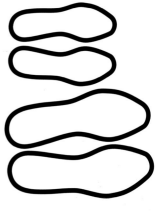

Templates for the shoe soles.

Materials and tools

You can make the sugar shoes using your usual sugarcraft materials and tools. You can buy the cutters for the shoe soles, which I have used, but you could use the templates provided on page 4 instead.

Materials

Non-stick workboard

Full-strength confectioner's varnish

Piping gel

Ready-coloured flower paste

Mexican paste (or use the recipe below)

Sugarpaste

Pearl and metallic edible powder food colours

Edible glitter

Edible stars

Tiny silver sugar balls

Small compartment craft box

Food colouring

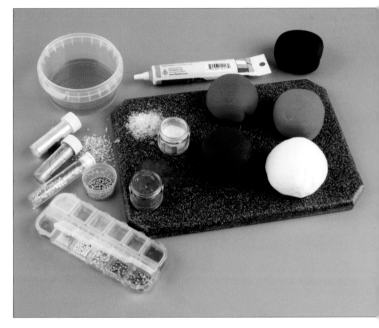

Mexican paste is a sugar modelling paste made with gum, which makes it stronger and allows it to be rolled out thinly. It dries slowly, going leathery before it dries hard. It is available commercially or can be made using the following recipe.

Mexican paste recipe

Place 225g (8oz) icing sugar into a bowl. Add three 5ml teaspoons of gum tragacanth. Mix the dry ingredients together. Add six 5ml teaspoons of cold water. Stir by hand until it becomes crumbly but damp enough to bind together. Add a little more water if too dry, or icing sugar if too wet. Turn out on to a worktop and knead until pliable. Place in a plastic food bag and leave at room temperature for twelve hours until firm.

Break off a small piece and knead between your palms. Continue kneading between your fingers. Repeat until all the paste is softened. The paste can be used straight away.

Store paste in an airtight container at room temperature, never in the fridge. If you have leftover paste, wrap each piece in cling film and place all of the pieces into a plastic food bag and place them in the freezer. Defrost only the quantity required for using. Smaller pieces will defrost more quickly.

Note: Mexican paste and flower paste can also be coloured by adding strong paste food colours. When making dark colours, the paste can become very soft, which is why I like to use ready-coloured black, red and purple paste.

Tools

Small non-stick rolling pin This is used for rolling out the paste.

Design wheel For adding large stitch and zigzag patterns and lines.

Quilting tool For adding small stitch patterns.

Cutting wheel This is used for cutting shapes from rolled paste.

Dresden tool This is used for marking holes, shaping paste and pressing on fluff or wool without flattening it.

Dogbone/ball tool For shaping the paste into rounded or cupped shapes.

Small fine palette knife This is used for releasing paste from the work surface and for cutting and marking lines.

Waterbrush/small paintbrush and water Used for dampening the paste before attaching pieces.

Petal veiner tool This is used to frill the Frilly Bootees on page 14.

Dowel The shoe soles are laid over a pen or pencil, acting as a dowel to create the high-heeled shape.

Small sharp pointed scissors For trimming ends of paste.

Tiny butterfly embosser Used to create a design on the Butterfly Shoes (page 8).

Real lace This was used to create the pattern on the Purple Lace Sandal on page 40. You could use a **fine lace embosser** if you have one.

Shoe sole, circle, square, ovals, leaf/petal, small fluted oval, heart and tiny star cutters

Dusting brush For applying edible powder food colour; I use a small blusher brush.

Music stave cutter For cutting out ribbon shapes.

Tea strainer/sieve Used to create fluff by pushing sugarpaste through the mesh.

Number one piping tube For embossing little holes.

Multi-mould with tiara, tiny flower and bow

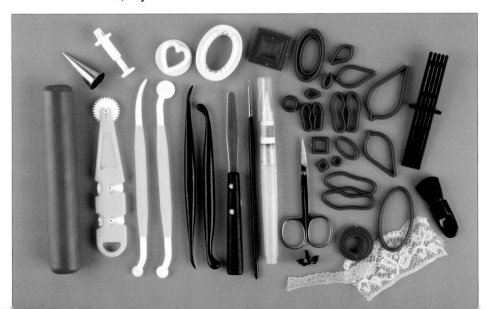

Butterfly Shoes

Materials:

Mexican paste/flower paste
White pearl edible powder food colour

Tools:

Small non-stick rolling pin
4cm (1½in) shoe sole cutter
2cm (¾in) heart cutter
Tiny butterfly embosser
2cm (¾in) and 1.5cm (⅝in) circle cutters
Dowel

Dresden tool
Music stave cutter
Dusting brush
Small fine palette knife
Small sharp pointed scissors
Waterbrush/small paintbrush and water

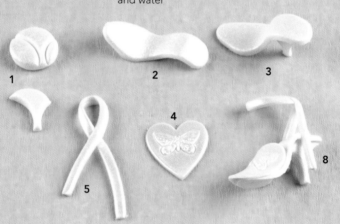

Instructions:

1 For the heel, roll out the paste to a thickness of 2mm ($^{1}/_{10}$in). Brush both sides with white pearl edible powder food colour. Cut the paste using the 1.5cm (⅝in) circle cutter. Use the 2cm (¾in) circle cutter to cut the smaller curve across the middle to form the back curve of the heel. Cut again using the 1.5cm (⅝in) circle to form the front curve. Allow the heel to dry for a few minutes, turning it over occasionally.

2 For the sole, roll the paste to 1mm ($^{1}/_{20}$in) thick. Brush both sides with white pearl edible powder. Cut out the 4cm (1½in) sole. Rest the heel of the sole over a dowel for a few minutes to create the curved, high-heeled shape, until the sole feels leathery.

3 Dampen the top curve of the heel and attach under the sole. Lay the shoe on its side and cut a tiny piece off the point of the heel to enable it to stand straight. Stand the shoe up and allow to dry for at least thirty minutes.

4 Roll out the paste thinly. Allow to dry slightly on each side until the paste feels leathery. Brush the surface with white pearl edible powder. Cut out the 2cm (¾in) heart. Emboss with the tiny butterfly cutter.

5 Cut the 8cm (3¹⁄₈in) strap from the rest of the rolled-out paste with the music stave cutter. Loop the strap as shown and dampen where the strap crosses to attach it to itself.

6 Dampen the underside edges of the heart shape and stick to the sides of the sole.

7 Dampen the side edges of the heel end of the sole. Press the ends of the strap on to the sides, overlapping the edges, holding the loop forwards. Lay the shoe on its side and cut off the excess strap ends with the sharp pointed scissors.

8 Stand the shoe up and allow to dry.

Madame Butterfly

You can decorate the butterfly with pink pearl edible powder, mixed with alcohol and applied with a fine paintbrush, or dust the shoes with different pearl or metallic powder colours.

Ballet Shoes

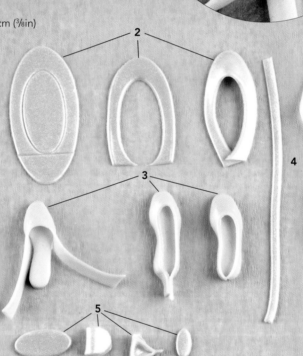

Materials:

Mexican paste/flower paste in pale
    peach or pale pink

White pearl edible powder food colour

Tools:

Small non-stick rolling pin

3cm (1¼in) shoe sole cutter

5cm (2in) and 3cm (1¼in)
    oval cutters

2cm (¾in) and 1cm (⅜in)
    oval cutters
    for bow

Music stave
    cutter

Dogbone/ball
    tool

Dusting brush

Small fine
    palette knife

Dresden tool

Small sharp
    pointed
    scissors

Waterbrush/
    small
    paintbrush
    and water

Instructions:

1 For the sole, roll out the paste to a thickness of 1mm (¹⁄₂₀in). Brush the surface with white pearl edible powder food colour. Cut out the 3cm (1¼in) sole. Allow to dry flat for at least thirty minutes, turning it over occasionally.

2 Roll out the paste thinly. Allow to dry slightly on each side until the paste feels leathery. Brush the surface with white pearl edible powder. Cut out a 5cm (2in) oval. Use the 3cm (1¼in) oval cutter to cut out the middle. Cut straight across at one end as shown and discard the middle oval and the end piece to create the shoe top. Use the dogbone/ball tool to cup the inside of the toe end.

3 Dampen the sides of the sole. Attach the top to the sole starting at the toe end, gently pressing the paste to the sides of the sole. Use the Dresden tool to help with shaping. Dampen the excess ends and press them together. Cut through the excess with sharp pointed scissors.

4 To make the bow and ribbons, roll out the paste very thinly. Allow to dry slightly on each side until the paste feels leathery. Brush both sides with white pearl edible powder. Cut out two 2cm (¾in) ovals and one 1cm (⅜in) oval for the bow. Cut four 8cm (3⅛in) ribbons from the rest of the rolled-out paste using the music stave cutter. Twirl the ribbons. For best results, attach the ribbons only when the shoes are in place on the cake. Dampen the inside edge of the shoes and attach the ribbons, positioning them as shown.

5 Make the bow by folding each of the 2cm (¾in) ovals in half and pinching the narrow end. Dampen the shoe ribbons where they cross and attach the two pinched ovals on top. Dampen the 1cm (⅜in) oval and press it in to the centre using the Dresden tool. Care should be taken when handling the finished shoes, as the ribbons are fragile.

Kitten Slipper

Materials:

Mexican paste/flower paste
  in pink

Pink sugarpaste for the fluff

Tools:

Small non-stick rolling pin

1cm (³⁄₈in) and 2.5cm (1in)
  circle cutters

4cm (1½in) shoe sole cutter

Dowel

Tea strainer/sieve

Small fine palette knife

Dresden tool

Waterbrush/small paintbrush
  and water

Instructions:

1 For the heel, roll out the paste to a thickness of 2mm (¹⁄₁₀in). Cut out a 1cm (³⁄₈in) circle. Use the same circle cutter to cut across the middle to form the back curve of the heel. Cut again to form the front curve. Allow the heel to dry for a few minutes, turning it over occasionally.

2 To make the sole, roll the Mexican paste to a thickness of 1mm (¹⁄₂₀in). Cut out the 4cm (1½in) sole. Rest the heel end of the sole over a dowel for a few minutes to create the high-heeled shape, until the sole feels leathery.

3 Dampen the top curve of the heel and attach under the sole. Lay the slipper on its side and cut a tiny piece off the point of the heel to enable it to stand straight. Stand the shoe up and allow to dry for at least thirty minutes.

4 Roll out the Mexican paste thinly. Allow to dry slightly on each side until the paste feels leathery. Cut out a 2.5cm (1in) circle. Use the same cutter to cut a tiny curve off for the toe end, and a larger piece off the other side of the circle. Dampen the underside edges of the shape and stick to the sides of the sole and allow to dry for at least thirty minutes.

5 To make the fluff, press small pea-sized pieces of pink sugarpaste through a tea strainer or sieve with your thumb or finger. Use the palette knife to remove the fluff. Dampen the surface of the toe piece. Use the Dresden tool or cocktail stick to attach the fluff without flattening it.

6 Stand the slipper up and allow to dry.

Frilly Bootees

Materials:

Mexican paste/flower paste in white and pale pink

White pearl edible powder food colour

Tools:

Small non-stick rolling pin

5cm (2in) oval cutter

3cm (1¼in) oval cutter

2.5cm (1in) circle cutter

Small fine palette knife

Petal veiner tool

Dresden tool

Dogbone/ball tool

Small sharp pointed scissors

Waterbrush/small paintbrush and water

Multi-mould with bow

Instructions:

1 To make the sole, roll out the white paste to a thickness of 2mm (¹/₁₀in). Brush both sides with white pearl edible powder food colour. Cut the paste using the 3cm (1¼in) oval cutter. Allow to dry for a few minutes.

2 Roll out the pink paste thinly. Allow to dry slightly on each side until the paste feels leathery. Brush the surface with white pearl edible powder.

3 Cut out a 2.5cm (1in) circle and a 5cm (2in) oval. Cut the oval in half lengthways.

4 For the frills, roll out the white paste thinly. Allow to dry slightly on each side until the paste feels leathery. Brush the surface with white pearl edible powder.

5 Cut out a 2.5cm (1in) circle and a 5cm (2in) oval. Roll the petal veiner tool firmly over the edges shown.

6 Use the same shape cutter to cut off the thin strip of frill. Dampen the edge of the underside of the pink circle and oval and attach the frills, trimming off any excess with sharp pointed scissors.

7 Use the dogbone/ball tool to cup the flat area of the circle. Dampen around the edge of the oval sole. Stick the pink frilly circle on first, leaving the frilly part curved up.

8 Use the dogbone/ ball tool to cup the frilly pink half-oval and wrap it round the back of the sole, dampening the front edges to stick on top of the front of the bootee.

9 To make the bow, push a very tiny piece of white paste into the bow mould. Take the bow out of the mould and brush it with white pearl edible powder. Dampen the back and press the bow on to the front of the bootee.

Little Boy Blue

You might of course need pale blue paste instead of pink. These bootees are the perfect cake topper for a baby shower or to celebrate a new arrival or christening.

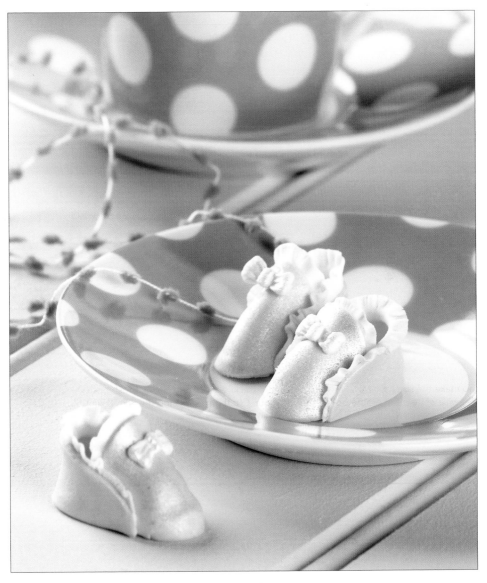

Strappy Sandal

Materials:

Small non-stick rolling pin

Mexican paste/flower
    paste in white and
    bright pink

Edible glitter

Tiny silver balls

Piping gel/edible glue

Tools:

4cm (1½in) shoe sole cutter

1.5cm (⅝in) and 2.5cm (1in)
    circle cutters

Dowel

Music stave cutter

Dresden tool

Small fine palette knife

Small sharp pointed scissors

Waterbrush /small paintbrush
    and water

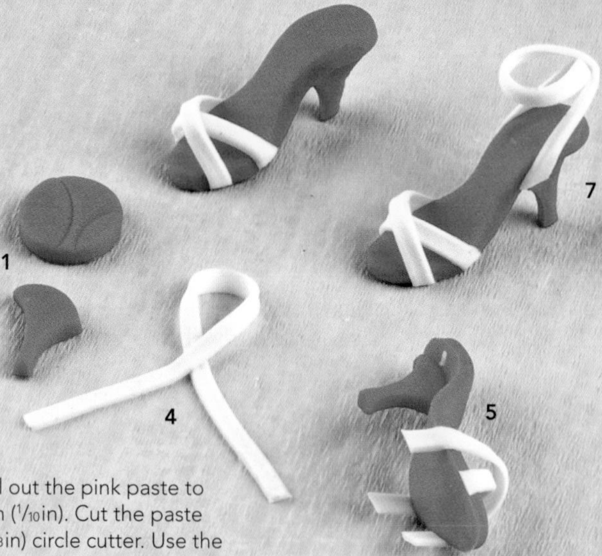

Instructions:

1 For the heel, roll out the pink paste to
a thickness of 2mm (¹⁄₁₀in). Cut the paste
using the 1.5cm (⅝in) circle cutter. Use the
2.5cm (1in) circle cutter to cut across the middle to form the
back curve of the heel. Cut again using the 1.5cm (⅝in) circle
to form the front curve. Allow the heel to dry for a few minutes, turning it
over occasionally.

2 Roll the pink paste to a thickness of 1mm (¹⁄₂₀in). Cut out the 4cm (1½in) sole. Rest
the heel end of the sole over a dowel for a few minutes to make the high-heeled shape,
until the sole feels leathery.

3 Dampen the top curve of the heel and attach under the sole. Lay the shoe on its side
and cut a tiny piece off the point of the heel using the palette knife to enable it to stand
straight. Stand the shoe up and allow to dry for at least thirty minutes.

4 Roll out the white paste thinly. Allow to dry slightly on each side until the paste feels
leathery. Cut the straps using the music stave cutter. Loop one strap as shown and
dampen where the strap crosses to attach it to itself.

5 Dampen the side edges of the front end of the sole. Press one strap to the sides, overhanging the edges. Repeat, crossing over the top of the first strap. Lay the shoe on its side and cut off the excess strap ends with the sharp pointed scissors.

6 Dampen the side edges of the heel end of the sole. Take the strap from step 4. Press the ends to the sides of the sole, overlapping the edges and holding the loop forwards. Cut the excess off as in step 5.

7 Stand the shoe up and allow to dry, until dry enough to hold by the heel.

8 Brush piping gel or edible glue over the straps. Sprinkle with edible glitter. Use a small, dry paintbrush or cotton bud to remove excess glitter.

9 Attach tiny silver balls with piping gel or edible glue.

Flip Flops

Materials:

Mexican paste/flower paste in
  white, purple and pink

Tools:

Small non-stick rolling pin

4cm (1½in) shoe sole cutter

2.5cm (1in) square cutter

Dresden tool

Multi-mould with tiny flower

Dogbone/ball tool

Small sharp pointed scissors

Waterbrush/small paintbrush
  and water

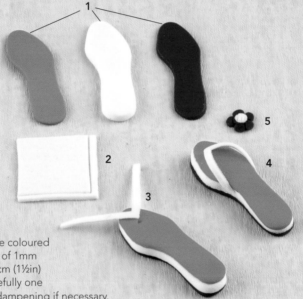

Instructions:

1 Roll out each of the coloured
pastes to a thickness of 1mm
($^1/_{20}$in). Cut out the 4cm (1½in)
soles. Stick them carefully one
on top of the other, dampening if necessary.

2 Roll out the white paste thinly. Allow to dry slightly on each side until the paste feels
leathery. Cut out the 2.5cm (1in) square. Move the cutter slightly to cut the 'v' shape.

3 Use the Dresden tool to make a small hole on the top of the sole where the toe post
would go. Dampen the hole. Dampen the sides of the sole where the straps will attach.

4 Lay the 'v' shape on the sole with the point over the hole. Press the point in with the
Dresden tool. Flip the straps over and stick them to the sides. Cut through the excess with
sharp pointed scissors.

5 For the flower, press a very tiny piece of white paste into the flower mould for the
textured centre. Press a tiny piece of the purple paste into the mould on top of the white,
using the dogbone/ball tool. The paste should only just come up to the surface of the
mould. Take the flower out of the mould straight away, dampen the back and stick it on to
the centre of the straps.

Beach Babe

Change the colours to suit the cake or celebration. You can also add more layers for a thicker, more stripy sole.

Baby Sneakers

Materials:

Mexican paste/flower paste in
white and dark blue

Tools:

Small non-stick rolling pin

5cm (2in), 3cm (1¼in) and
2cm (¾in) oval cutters

2.5cm (1in) circle cutter

Small fine palette knife

Cutting wheel

Waterbrush/small
paintbrush
and water

Dogbone/ball tool

Quilting tool

Small sharp pointed scissors

Music stave cutter

Tiny star cutter

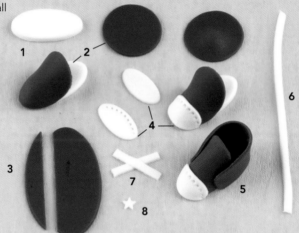

Instructions:

1 For the sole, roll out the white paste to 2mm (¹/₁₀in) thick. Cut out a 3cm (1¼in) oval.

2 Roll out blue paste thinly. Cut out a 2.5cm (1in) circle and a 5cm (2in) oval. Use a dogbone/ball tool to cup one end of the circle. Dampen around the side edge of the sole. Attach the front of the sneaker at the toe end. The top needs to curve upwards.

3 Use the cutting wheel to cut off a strip of about 2mm (¹/₁₀in) from the long side of the oval and discard it.

4 Roll out the white paste thinly. Cut out a 2cm (¾in) oval. Emboss a stitch pattern with the quilting tool along one edge. Stick to the front of the sneaker for the toe.

5 Dampen along the straight edge of the blue cut oval made in step 3 and wrap it round the back of the sole, overlapping the front of the sneaker.

6 Cut strips of white paste using the music stave cutter. Dampen the bottom edge of the sneaker and wrap one of the strips round the base. Join it at the back and cut off the excess with sharp pointed scissors.

7 Cut two of the strips to approximately 1cm (³⁄₈in) long. Make a wide 'x' by dampening and crossing them over, then attach to the front of the sneaker to look like laces. Cut off the excess with sharp pointed scissors.

8 Cut out a tiny white star and stick it to the side of the sneaker.

Cool Baby!
Make sneakers in your own choice of colours. They would look great on a first birthday cake.

Football Boots

Materials:

Mexican paste/flower paste in white and orange

Tiny silver balls

Piping gel/edible glue

Tools:

Small non-stick rolling pin

3cm (1¼in) shoe sole cutter

5cm (2in) and 2cm (¾in) oval cutters

1.5cm (⅝in) square cutter

Quilting tool

Small fine palette knife

Dresden tool

Small sharp pointed scissors

Waterbrush/small paintbrush and water

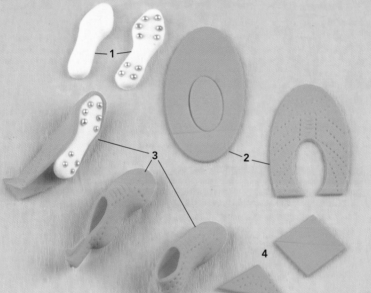

Instructions:

1 Roll out the white paste to a thickness of 1mm (¹⁄₂₀in). Cut out the 3cm (1¼in) sole. Make holes for the studs using the Dresden tool. Dot a tiny amount of piping gel or edible glue in each hole. Stick tiny silver balls into the holes and press them in gently. Allow to dry flat for at least thirty minutes, turning it over occasionally.

2 Roll out the orange paste thinly. Allow it to dry slightly on each side until the paste feels leathery. Cut out the 5cm (2in) oval and 1.5cm (⅝in) square. Use the 2cm (¾in) oval cutter to cut out the middle towards one end of the large oval and discard it. Cut straight across at the end as shown using the palette knife. Mark lines and dots to represent the laces using the palette knife and Dresden tool. Mark small stitches using the quilting tool.

3 Dampen the sides of the sole. Attach the top to the sole starting at the toe end, gently pressing the paste carefully to the sides of the sole. Use the Dresden tool to help shape the boot from the inside. Dampen the ends and press them together. Cut through the excess with sharp pointed scissors.

4 Cut the 1.5cm (⁵⁄₈in) square in half diagonally with the palette knife and mark stitching round the edge using the quilting tool. Dampen the underside and wrap around the back of the boot.

Elf Boots

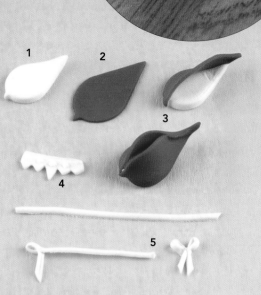

Materials:

Mexican paste/flower paste
  in white and red
Tiny silver balls
Piping gel/edible glue

Tools:

Small non-stick rolling pin
3cm (1¼in) and 4cm (1½in)
  leaf/petal cutters
Multi-mould tiara
Music stave cutter
Dresden tool
Small sharp pointed
  scissors
Waterbrush/small
  paintbrush and water

Instructions:

1 Roll out the white paste to a thickness of 1mm (¹⁄₂₀in). Cut out a 3cm (1¼in) leaf/petal shape for the sole.

2 Roll out the red paste thinly. Allow to dry slightly on each side until the paste feels leathery. Cut out two 4cm (1½in) leaf/petal shapes.

3 Dampen the sides of the sole. Attach the red leaf/petal shapes to the sole, starting at the toe end, gently pressing the paste carefully to the sides of the sole. Use the Dresden tool to help shape the boot from the inside. Dampen the heel end and along the top at the front and press together, leaving the wide end open on top.

4 Make two white tiaras from the multi-mould using white paste. Stick them around the top of the boot with the points facing down.

5 Roll out the white paste thinly. Leave it to dry for a few minutes until it feels leathery, turning it over occasionally. Cut out a short strip using the music stave cutter. Dampen a point a little way along the strip. Form a tiny loop and tail by bringing the end over to the dampened point, press in and bend the tail away from the loop. Repeat, bringing the other end in to the same point to form another loop and tail. Cut the tails to the length you want using sharp pointed scissors. Dampen the back of the boot to attach the bow.

24

6 Glue some tiny silver sugar balls to the point of the shoe with a little piping gel or edible glue.

Elfin Fashion
You could also make the boot in brown with tiny gold balls and mark lace holes with a no. 1 piping tube. Cut the zigzag top with sharp pointed scissors.

Patriotic Platforms

Materials:

Mexican paste/flower paste in white, red and blue
White edible glitter
Piping gel/edible glue

Tools:

Small non-stick rolling pin
4cm (1½in) shoe sole cutter
2.5cm (1in) circle cutter
Dowel
2cm (¾in) square cutter
Small fine palette knife

Music stave cutter
Dresden tool
Small sharp pointed
  scissors
Waterbrush/small
  paintbrush and water

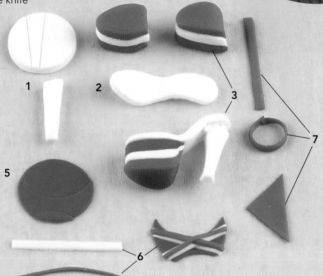

Instructions:

1 Roll out the white paste to a thickness of 2mm (¹⁄₁₀in). Cut out a 2.5cm (1in) circle. Cut across the middle with the palette knife. Cut again at a slight angle as shown; the curve on top helps to shape the sole. Allow the heel to dry for about thirty minutes, turning it over occasionally.

2 Roll the white paste to a thickness of 1mm (¹⁄₂₀in). Cut out the 4cm (1½in) sole. Rest the heel end over a dowel for a few minutes to create the high-heeled shape, until the sole feels leathery.

3 To make the platform sole, roll out the different coloured pastes to a thickness of 2mm (¹⁄₁₀in) thick. Use the shoe sole cutter to cut out just the wide, front part of the shoe in each colour. Carefully stick them on top of each other. Cut the already cut end, angling downwards to join the ends together. Turn the platform over and stick it to the underside of the sole. Lay it on its side and attach the heel. Stand the shoe up, making sure it stands straight. If necessary, the end of the heel should still be soft enough to cut. Leave to dry for about thirty minutes.

4 Brush piping gel or edible glue over the heel. Sprinkle with edible glitter. Use a small, dry paintbrush or cotton bud to remove excess glitter.

5 Roll out the blue paste thinly. Allow to dry slightly on each side until the paste feels leathery. Cut out a 2.5cm (1in) circle. Use the same cutter to cut a tiny curve off for the toe end and a larger piece off the other side of the circle.

6 Roll out the white and red paste thinly. Allow to dry slightly on each side until the paste feels leathery. Cut strips of each colour using the music stave cutter. Use the cutter to cut the red strip again to make it thinner than the white one. Stick the white strip across the top of the blue shape to form a wide 'X', then dampen and lay the thinner red strip over the top. Use the Dresden tool to help with shaping. Dampen the underside edges of the blue shape, stick to the sides of the sole and allow to dry for a few minutes.

7 For the back piece of the shoe, roll out the red paste thinly. Allow to dry slightly on each side until the paste feels leathery. Cut out a 2cm (¾in) square. Cut it in half diagonally. Use the Dresden tool to help with shaping, then dampen the long edge and stick it around the back of the heel end of the sole. Cut the 8cm (3⅛in) ankle strap from the rest of the rolled-out red paste, using the music stave cutter. Loop the strap to make a circle as shown and dampen it to attach it to the top of the triangle.

Star Spangled Stunner

Tiny edible stars could be stuck on to the blue toe piece using piping gel, to celebrate all things American.

Roman Sandals

Materials:

Mexican paste/flower
    paste in beige or
    old gold
Gold edible powder
    food colour
Tiny silver balls
Piping gel/edible glue

Tools:

Small non-stick rolling pin
4cm (1½in) shoe sole cutter
Music stave cutter
Dusting brush
Small fine palette knife
Dresden tool
Small sharp pointed scissors
Waterbrush/small paintbrush
    and water

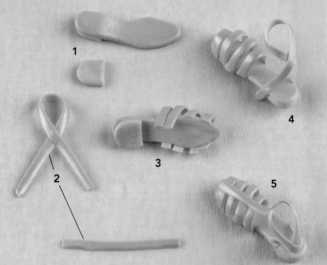

Instructions:

1 Roll out the paste to a thickness of 1mm (¹⁄₂₀in). Brush the surface with gold edible powder. Cut two 4cm (1½in) soles and cut off only the heel part of one of them. Stick the heel under the sole. Allow to dry for at least thirty minutes, turning it over occasionally.

2 For the straps, roll out the paste thinly. Brush the surface with gold edible powder. Allow to dry slightly on each side until the paste feels leathery. Cut straps using the music stave cutter: four 4cm (1½in) long for the front, one 4cm (1½in) long for the vertical strap, and one 8cm (3⅛in) long for the ankle strap. Loop the ankle strap as shown and dampen where the strap crosses to attach it to itself.

3 Dampen the sides of the sole. Attach the front straps starting at the toe end, by gently pressing the paste carefully to the sides of the sole, overlapping the edges. Cut through the excess with sharp pointed scissors.

4 Dampen the sides of the heel end of the sole. Press the ends of the ankle strap to the sides, overlapping the edges, holding the loop forwards. Lay the shoe on its side and cut off the excess strap ends with the pointed scissors.

5 Dampen down the middle of the front and ankle straps. Stick the vertical strap on, starting at the toe end and finishing at the ankle strap.

6 Attach tiny silver balls using piping gel or edible glue.

Zebra Wedge

Materials:

Mexican paste/flower
   paste in black and white

Tools:

Small non-stick rolling pin

4cm (1½in) shoe sole cutter

2.5cm (1in) circle cutter

Small fine palette knife

Cutting wheel

Music stave cutter

Dresden tool

Small sharp pointed scissors

Waterbrush/small paintbrush
   and water

Instructions:

1 For the platform wedge, roll out the
two pastes to about 2mm (¹⁄₁₀in) thick.
Use the sole cutter to cut out just the
narrow, heel part in each colour (two of each). Carefully stick them on
top of each other. Cut the already cut end, angling downwards to
join the ends together.

2 Roll out the black and white pastes to the thickness of
1mm (¹⁄₂₀in) and cut out a sole from each. Stick the wedge
heel on top of the black sole. Attach the white insole over
the top of the heel and sole. Allow to dry for at least thirty
minutes, turning it over occasionally.

3 For the front, roll out the white and black paste thinly.
Use the cutting wheel to cut tiny irregular-shaped black
strips. Lay them over the white paste to form a zebra
pattern and roll over with a rolling pin to fuse the colours
together. Cut out a 2.5cm (1in) circle. Use the same cutter
to cut a tiny curve off for the toe end and a larger piece off
the other side of the circle. Dampen the underside edges of the
shape and stick to the sides of the toe end of the sole.

4 For the ankle straps, roll out the black paste thinly. Allow it to dry slightly on each side until the paste feels leathery. Cut straps using the music stave cutter.

5 Dampen the side edges of the heel end of the sole. Press the ends of the straps to the sides, twirl the straps together and lay them down on one side of the shoe. Cut off the excess strap ends with the sharp pointed scissors.

Sheepskin Boot

Materials:

Mexican paste/flower paste
  in beige

Cream coloured sugarpaste

Tools:

Small non-stick rolling pin

5cm (2in) and 3cm (1¼in)
  oval cutters

2.5cm (1in) circle cutter

2.5cm (1in) square cutter

Small fine palette knife

Sieve/tea strainer

Waterbrush/small
  paintbrush and water

Dogbone/ball tool

Dresden tool

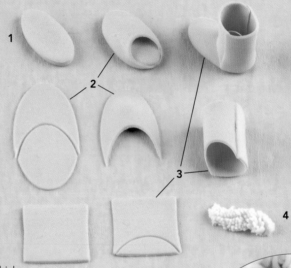

Instructions:

1 Roll out the beige
paste to 2mm (¹/₁₀in) thick.
Cut out a 3cm (1¼in) oval for the sole.

2 Roll out beige paste thinly. Cut out a 5cm (2in) oval
and two 2.5cm (1in) squares. Cut the oval again using
the same cutter as shown. Use a dogbone/ball tool to
cup the toe end of the oval. Dampen around the side
edge of the sole. Attach the front of the boot to the
sole, starting from the toe end.

3 Cut a curved edge on one of the squares using the
2.5cm (1in) circle cutter. Dampen along the two opposite
straight edges and attach the other square to form a
tube. Dampen around the back of the sole and press the
tube shape into place with the curved part joining the curved
part of the front of the boot.

4 Dampen the joins and the top edge of the boot. Use a sieve
or tea strainer to make the wool by pressing small amounts of cream
sugarpaste through it. Cut off the wool with a palette knife and attach it to the
dampened parts. Press into place with a Dresden tool to avoid flattening the wool.

Leopard Shoe

Materials:

Mexican paste/flower paste in black and beige

Dark brown and autumn leaf food colouring

Tools:

Small non-stick rolling pin

4cm (1½in) shoe
   sole cutter

2.5cm (1in) and 1.5cm
   (⅝in) circle cutters

2.5cm (1in) square cutter

Dowel

Small fine palette knife

Cutting wheel

Dresden tool

Dogbone/ball tool

Small sharp pointed
   scissors

Waterbrush/small
   paintbrush and water

Small fine paintbrush for painting

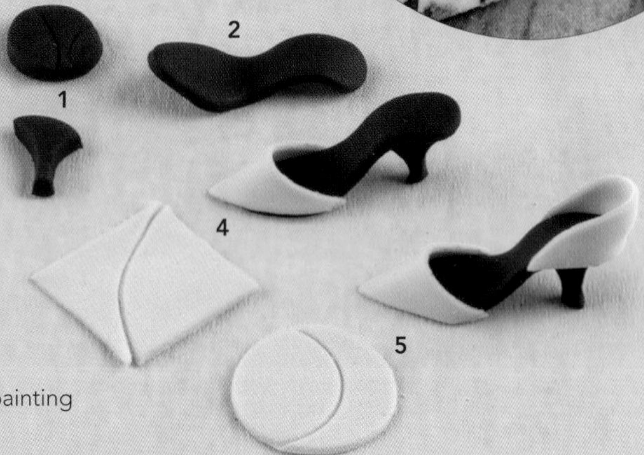

Instructions:

1 Roll out the black paste to a thickness of 2mm (¹/₁₀in). Cut out a 1.5cm (⅝in) circle. Use the 2.5cm (1in) circle cutter to cut across the middle to form the back curve of the heel. Cut again using the 1.5cm (⅝in) circle cutter to form the front curve of the heel. Allow the heel to dry for a few minutes, turning it over occasionally.

2 Roll out the black paste to a thickness of 1mm (¹/₂₀in). Cut out the 4cm (1½in) sole. Rest the heel end over a dowel for a few minutes to create the high-heeled look, until the sole feels leathery.

3 Dampen the top curve of the heel and attach under the sole. Lay the shoe on its side and cut a tiny piece off the point of the heel to enable it to stand straight. Stand the shoe up and allow to dry for at least thirty minutes.

4 Roll out the beige paste thinly. Allow to dry slightly on each side until the paste feels leathery. Cut out a 2.5cm (1in) square and a 2.5cm (1in) circle. Use the cutting wheel to cut across the square diagonally with a slight curve. Dampen the straight edges underneath and stick them to the sides of the sole to make the toe piece of the shoe.

5 Using the 2.5cm (1in) circle cutter, cut the beige circle to make a crescent moon shape for the shoe back. Cup the inside with the dogbone/ball tool. Dampen the inside curve underneath and attach it to the back of the sole.

6 To create the leopard spots, paint tiny, roughly circular outlines of dark brown all over the beige parts, and then fill the outlines with autumn leaf colouring. Allow to dry.

Dorothy Shoes

Materials:

Mexican paste/flower
   paste in black and red
Edible red glitter
Piping gel/edible glue

Tools:

Small non-stick rolling pin
4cm (1½in) shoe sole cutter
1cm (³⁄₈in) circle cutter
5cm (2in) oval cutter
Small fine palette knife
Cutting wheel
Dogbone/ball tool
Dresden tool
Small sharp pointed scissors
Waterbrush/small paintbrush
   and water

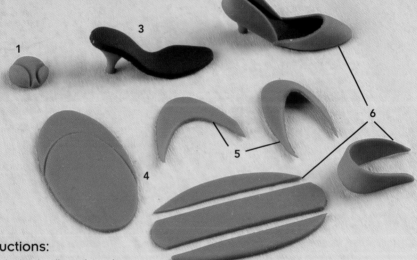

Instructions:

1 For the heel, roll out the red paste
to a thickness of 2mm (¹⁄₁₀in). Cut the
paste using the 1cm (³⁄₈in) circle cutter. Use the same cutter to cut across the middle to form
the back curve of the heel. Cut again to form the front curve of the heel. Allow the heel to
dry for a few minutes, turning it over occasionally.

2 Roll out the black paste to a thickness of 1mm (¹⁄₂₀in). Cut out the 4cm (1½in) sole. Rest
the heel of the sole over a dowel for a few minutes, until the sole feels leathery.

3 Dampen the top curve of the heel and attach under the sole. Lay the shoe on its side and
cut a tiny piece off the point of the heel with the sharp pointed scissors to enable it to stand
straight. Stand the shoe up and allow to dry for at least thirty minutes.

4 Roll out the red paste thinly. Allow to dry slightly on each side until the paste feels
leathery. Cut out two 5cm (2in) ovals.

5 On one of the ovals use the same cutter to cut a curve off for the toe end, as shown. Cup the toe end with the dogbone/ball tool. Dampen the underside edges of the shape and stick to the sides of the sole.

6 For the shoe back, cut a 1cm (⅜in) strip out of the middle of the other oval, and discard that piece. Cup one of the curved pieces with the dogbone/ball tool. Dampen the straight edge and attach to the back to the sole. Allow to dry.

7 Brush a thin layer of piping gel or edible glue all over the red parts of the shoe and sprinkle with edible red glitter. Allow to dry.

Black Brogue

Materials:

Mexican paste/flower paste
in black

Confectioner's varnish/
piping gel

Tools:

Small non-stick rolling pin

4cm (1½in) and 3cm (1¼in)
shoe sole cutters

3cm (1¼in) and 1cm (⅜in)
oval cutters

3cm (1¼in) leaf/petal cutter

Quilting tool

Palette knife

Dresden tool

Cutting wheel

Small sharp pointed scissors

Waterbrush/small paintbrush
and water

Cotton bud if using
confectioner's varnish

Instructions:

1 Roll out the paste to a thickness of 1mm (¹⁄₂₀in). Cut out two 3cm (1¼in) soles and cut just the heel part off one of them. Stick the heel on to the sole. Allow to dry for at least thirty minutes, turning it over occasionally.

2 Roll out the paste thinly. Allow to dry slightly on each side until the paste feels leathery. Cut out two of the 4cm (1½in) soles and one 3cm (1¼in) oval. To make the top, on one of the soles cut a line from the heel to the middle. Dampen the sides of the sole. Attach the top to the sole starting at the toe end, gently pressing the paste carefully to the sides of the sole. Use the Dresden tool if necessary to help with shaping the inside. Dampen the excess ends and press them together. Cut through the excess with sharp pointed scissors.

3 For the stitched piece, use the cut-out 3cm (1¼in) oval and cut one end off using the same oval cutter. Cut the middle of the shape with the 1cm (⅜in) oval cutter. Cut a line to the middle as shown. Run the quilting tool around the edge for stitching and mark laces with a knife. Stick it on top of the shoe with the split at the heel end.

4 On the remaining sole shape cut the toe end to shape using the leaf/petal cutter. Mark stitches round the edge with the quilting tool. Stick to the front of the shoe.

5 The shoe can be made to shine by painting either with confectioner's varnish using a cotton bud, or with piping gel using a small paintbrush.

Purple Lace Sandal

Materials:

Mexican paste/flower paste in purple
Edible gold powder food colour
Edible gold stars

Tools:

Small non-stick rolling pin
4cm (1½in) shoe sole cutter
2.5cm (1in) and 2cm (¾in) circle cutters
Dowel
Small piece of real lace/fine lace embosser
Small fine palette knife
Cutting wheel
Dresden tool
Small sharp pointed scissors
Waterbrush/small paintbrush
   and water
Dusting brush

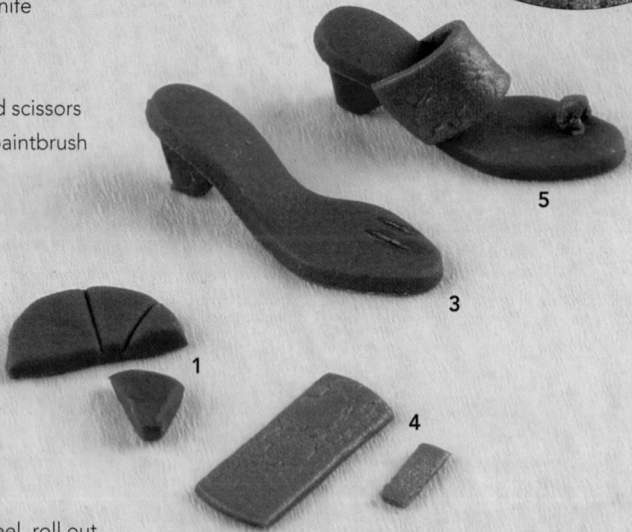

Instructions:

1 For the Cuban heel, roll out
the paste to a thickness of 2mm
(¹⁄₁₀in). Cut the paste using the 2cm (¾in) circle
cutter. Cut across the top of the circle as shown,
then cut the heel shape using the palette knife.
Allow the heel to dry for a few minutes, turning it over occasionally.

2 Roll the paste to a thickness of 1mm (¹⁄₂₀in). Cut out the 4cm (1½in) sole. Rest the
heel end of the sole over a dowel for a few minutes to create the high-heeled shape,
until the sole feels leathery.

3 Dampen the top curve of the heel and attach under the sole. Lay the shoe on its
side and cut a tiny piece off the point of the heel to enable it to stand straight. Mark
with the palette knife where the toe strap will go. Stand the shoe up and allow to dry
for at least thirty minutes.

4 To make the top and toe strap, roll out the paste thinly. Allow to dry slightly on each side until the paste feels leathery. Cut out a 2.5cm (1in) circle. Press the lace on top with a rolling pin or use a fine lace embossser. Cut a 1cm (³/₈in) wide strip across the embossed circle, then cut a strip 1 x 3mm (³/₈ x ¹/₈in) from the leftover embossed pieces. Brush both lightly with edible gold powder. Dampen the marks on the sole for the toe strap and attach it.

5 Dampen the underside edges of the top and attach it to the sides of the sole.

6 Brush a thin layer of piping gel or edible glue over the top edge and sprinkle it with edible gold stars. Attach one gold star to the toe strap. Allow to dry.

Men's Slippers

Materials:

Mexican paste/flower paste
    in brown

Dark green edible powder
    food colour

Tools:

Small non-stick rolling pin

3cm (1¼in) oval cutter

2.5cm (1in) circle cutter

Small fine palette knife

Music stave cutter

Waterbrush or small
    paintbrush and water

Design wheel

Dusting brush

Instructions:

1 Roll out the paste to a thickness of 2mm (¹/₁₀in). Cut out a 3cm (1¼in) oval to make the sole of the slipper.

2 Roll out the paste thinly. Cut out a 2.5cm (1in) circle.

3 Emboss lines on the circle using the music stave cutter.

4 Use the dusting brush to colour the raised surface with dark green edible powder food colour. The embossed lines will stay brown if you only use a small amount of colour.

5 Mark stitches around half of the circle using the design wheel. Dampen around the side edge of the sole. Attach the front of the slipper from the toe end.

Patent Party Shoe

Materials:

Mexican paste/flower paste in black
Confectioner's varnish/piping gel

Tools:

Small non-stick rolling pin
4cm (1½in) shoe sole cutter
2.5cm (1in) and 1.5cm (⅝in)
   circle cutters
Dowel
2.5cm (1in) square cutter
3.5cm (1⅜in) fluted oval cutter
Dogbone/ball tool
Small fine palette knife

Number one piping tube
Cutting wheel
Dresden tool
Small sharp pointed scissors
Waterbrush/small paintbrush and water
Music stave cutter
Cotton bud for varnishing

Instructions:

1 For the heel, roll out the paste to a thickness of 2mm (¹⁄₁₀in). Cut out the paste using the 1.5cm (⅝in) circle cutter. Use the 2.5cm (1in) circle cutter to cut across the middle to form the back curve of the heel. Cut again using the 1.5cm (⅝in) circle to form the front curve. Allow the heel to dry for a few minutes, turning it over occasionally.

2 Roll the black paste to a thickness of 1mm (¹⁄₂₀in). Cut out the 4cm (1½in) sole. Rest the heel end of the sole over a dowel for a few minutes, until the sole feels leathery.

3 Dampen the top curve of the heel and attach under the sole. Lay the shoe on its side and cut a tiny piece off the point of the heel using sharp pointed scissors, to enable it to stand straight. Stand the shoe up and allow to dry for at least thirty minutes.

4 Roll out the paste thinly. Allow to dry slightly on each side until the paste feels leathery. Cut out a 2.5cm (1in) square and a 3.5cm (1⅜in) fluted oval.

5 Use the fluted oval cutter to cut across the square diagonally. Emboss little holes using the number one piping tube. Dampen the underside straight edges and stick to the sides of the sole.

6 Using the fluted oval piece, cut a narrow strip down the centre of the oval. Cup one of the half-moon shapes with the dogbone/ball tool. Dampen the non-fluted edge and attach to the back of the sole.

7 Cut a strap using the music stave cutter. Cut it to fit for the ankle strap. Dampen the inside of the enclosed heel and attach the strap, pressing it into place with the Dresden tool. Stand the shoe up and allow to dry. It can be made to shine either by painting with confectioner's varnish using a cotton bud, or with piping gel using a small paintbrush.

Diagonal Sandal

Materials:

Mexican paste/flower paste in white and blue
Gold and white pearl edible powder
    food colours

Tools:

Small non-stick rolling pin
4cm (1½in) shoe sole cutter
Dusting brush
1.5cm (⅝in) circle cutter
Dowel
Dresden tool
Music stave cutter
Small fine palette knife
Small sharp pointed
    scissors
Waterbrush/small
    paintbrush and water

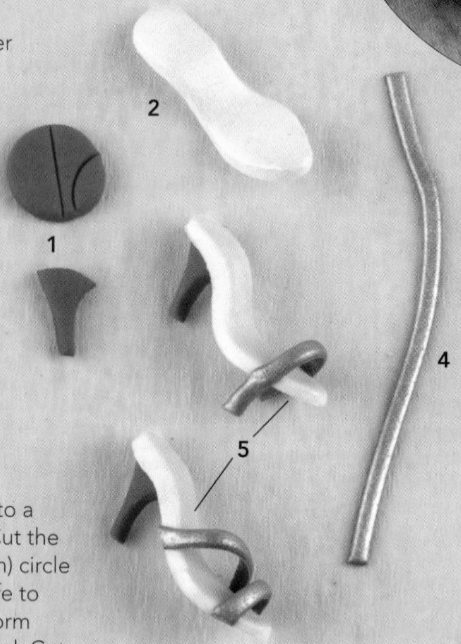

Instructions:

1 Roll out the blue paste to a
thickness of 2mm (¹⁄₁₀in). Cut the
paste using the 1.5cm (⅝in) circle
cutter. Use the palette knife to
cut across the middle to form
the straight back of the heel. Cut
again using the 1.5cm (⅝in) circle
cutter to form the front curve.
Allow the heel to dry for a few minutes, turning it over occasionally.

2 For the sole, roll the white paste to a thickness of 1mm (¹⁄₂₀in). Brush over the surface
with edible gold powder. Cut out the 4cm (1½in) sole. Rest the heel end of the sole over
a dowel for a few minutes to create the high-heeled shape, until the sole feels leathery.

3 Dampen the top curve of the heel and attach it under the sole. Lay the shoe on its
side and cut a tiny piece off the point of the heel using the sharp pointed scissors, to
enable it to stand straight. Stand the shoe up and allow to dry for at least thirty minutes.

4 Roll out the blue paste thinly. Brush over the surface with edible white pearl powder.
Allow to dry slightly on each side until the paste feels leathery. Cut the straps using the
music stave cutter.

5 Dampen the side edges of the front end of the sole. Press one strap to the sides,
overhanging the edges. Repeat, positioning the second strap diagonally up the shoe.
Lay the shoe on its side and cut off the excess strap ends with the pointed scissors.

46

Acknowledgements

My thanks to all at Search Press and to
Debbie Patterson for the photography.

Publisher's Note

If you would like more information about
sugarcraft, try the following books by the
same author, all published by Search Press:

Twenty to Make Sugar Animals
Twenty to Make Sugar Birds
Twenty to Make Sugar Fairies
Sensational Sugar Animals

You are invited to visit the
author's website:
www.franklysweet.co.uk
for more information and
video tutorials.